Truly Foul & Cheesy™
Animal Jokes & Facts

Published in Great Britain in MMXVII by
Book House, an imprint of
The Salariya Book Company Ltd
25 Marlborough Place, Brighton BN1 1UB
www.salariya.com

ISBN: 978-1-912006-54-0

SALARIYA

1 3 5 7 9 8 6 4 2

A CIP catalogue record for this book is available
from the British Library.

Printed and bound in China.
Printed on paper from sustainable sources.

Created and designed by
David Salariya.

Visit
www.salariya.com
for our online catalogue and
free fun stuff.

PAPER FROM
SUSTAINABLE
FORESTS

Author:
John Townsend worked as a
secondary school teacher before
becoming a full-time writer.
He specialises in illuminating and
humorous information books for
all ages.

Artist:
David Antram studied at
Eastbourne College of Art and then
worked in advertising for 15 years
before becoming a full-time artist.
He has illustrated many children's
non-fiction books.

Truly Foul & Cheesy™

Animal Jokes & Facts

This Truly Foul & Cheesy
book belongs to:

....

Written by

John Townsend

Illustrated by

David Antram

BOOK HOUSE
a SALARIYA imprint

Introduction

What's that scratching my back?

Warning – reading this book might not make you LOL (laugh out loud) but it could make you GOL (groan out loud), feel sick out loud or SEL (scream even louder). If you're reading this in a library by a SILENCE sign… get ready to be thrown out for LOL-GOL-SEL!

The author really hasn't made anything up in this book (apart from some daft limericks and jokes).

He checked out the foul facts as best he could and even double-checked the fouler bits to make absolutely sure – so please don't get too upset if you find out something different or meet a world famous mad scientist/historian/total genius who happens to know better.

'If I had my way, I'd RATify the lot!'

5

Who am I?

I'm **ENORMOUSLY** strong and intelligent
And, though you might think it's irrelevant,
I remember your smell,
Your appearance as well...
I never forget – 'cos I'm an elephant...
Oops, I forgot this was a riddle!

An elephant walks with a lollop,
Bashing trees with a lumbering wallop.
As it munches on leaves,
Its posterior heaves...
Quick – run for it...
Its tail lifts – and then the
BIG DOLLOP!

Can anyone answer this riddle?

I'm massive right round all my middle.
That's plenty of metres,
But it's two hundred litres
(Seven litres a second) when I piddle.

Yes, I'm an African elephant.

8

What about some elephant riddles?

What do you call an
elephant that never washes?
A smellyphant

What do you get if you cross
an elephant with a kangaroo?

Big holes all over Australia.

What do you get if you cross an elephant with
a peanut butter sandwich?

Either a sandwich that never forgets, or an
elephant that sticks to the roof of your mouth!

Q. What's grey, stands in a river when it rains and doesn't get wet?
A. An elephant with an umbrella

Q. What's grey and moves at a hundred miles an hour?
A. A jet propelled elephant

Q. Why do elephants never forget?
A. Because nobody ever tells them anything

Q. Why are elephants wrinkled?
A. Have you ever tried to iron one?

For the record: An elephant can urinate nearly 200 litres in one go (42 gallons). The sudden power-jet from its rear end is a bit like an almighty gush from a broken sewer pipe, as almost 7 litres (that's nearly 1.5 gallons) of liquid spurts out every second. You really didn't need to know that, did you? (Unless you plan to be walking behind an elephant any time soon.)

WARNING STINK ALERT

African elephants are amazing animals but beware...stand clear.

Elephants poo a huge amount all day and night. The amount of dung dumped by an adult elephant each day is a real stinker.

The average elephant squeezes out about 100kg (220 pounds) of sloppy poo every single day. That's about the same weight as a giant panda, a tiger, a lion, a gorilla or a new born elephant. Without wishing to kick up a stink, that's **HUGE** – over 200 times more than a human poos a day.

Impressed? It's certainly not to be sniffed at!

What happens to all this dung? Turn to page 12 to discover the foul facts of the disgusting dung beetle.

Many creatures make piles of poo their home, including beetles, scorpions, crickets and millipedes. Lured in by their taste for creepy-crawlies, several species of frog come hopping to poo piles to set up home. As well as creating a highly-nutritious residence for many smaller creatures, dung benefits animals that want to eat them. Honey badgers and meerkats will happily paw through dung piles to snack on the bugs and grubs hidden within.

The master of 'dung management' is that king of recycling; the dung beetle. Hold tight for a few foul facts:

- Some dung beetles ride on elephants and at the first 'plop' they hop off to tuck in to dinner. Other dung beetles will quickly arrive once they get a whiff of a delicious steamy supper ready and waiting.

I always get a takeaway at the weekend (more like a rollaway)

- Some dung beetles stay put in the poo and chomp away, while others prefer a take-away. They roll up a ball of poo and push it off to their nest to feed the babies. Dung beetle nests are packed with poo, and the female usually lays each egg in its own tiny dung sausage.

- Even a small ball of fresh dung can be hefty to push, weighing 50 times the weight of the beetle. One dung beetle can bury dung that is 250 times heavier than itself in one night.

- Fresh is best. Dung beetles like to strike while dinner is hot. Once an elephant dollop has dried out, it's not so appetising – even to the most dedicated poo eater. So dung beetles move in as soon as an elephant lifts its tail. Scientists have observed 4,000 dung beetles on a fresh pile of elephant scat within 15 minutes after it hit the ground. Within minutes, they were joined by 12,000 more dung beetles.

- A pile of elephant dung can vanish in two hours when thousands of dung beetles arrive on the scene to collect a piece of the action. Yummmm – anyone feeling hungry?!

Rat 1: How do you know if an elephant has been in the fridge?

Rat 2: Squashed tomatoes, flattened cheese and footprints in the butter. Anyway, you can't get an elephant in the fridge.

Rat 1: It's easy – just three steps. 1. Open fridge. 2. Put elephant in. 3. Close fridge.

Rat 2: Isn't that just the same for getting anything in the fridge?

Rat 1: Not quite. It's more complicated getting a giraffe in the fridge.

Rat 2: Why's that?

Rat 1: It's four steps. 1. Open fridge. 2. Take elephant out. 3. Put giraffe in. 4. Close fridge.

Rat 2: That's really cheesy.

Rat 1: No it's not. There's no cheese involved. The elephant ate it all.

Rat 2: Okay, then – there's a big party at the zoo. Which animal doesn't go and why?

Rat 1: That's easy – the giraffe. Its neck is stuck in the fridge.

Rat 2: Doh!

Watch Out –

Hippopotamus Alert!

Beware of a cross Hippopotamus
As it wallows in swamps that are bottomless...
Yet its own bottom's whopping,
As it shoots out a dropping...
Watch out – it'll splodge on the lot of us!

Keep away!

15

5 Hippo Facts

- The hippopotamus is the third largest land mammal (after the rhinoceros and elephant). It can be far grumpier, though.

- Hippopotamuses give birth in water. At least it saves time on giving baby a bath!

- Although hippos might look chubby with short legs, they can easily outrun a human. Hippos can be very aggressive, especially if they feel threatened and even though they won't eat you, a hippo can open its mouth wide enough to fit you inside. Those big teeth are deadly – making the hippo one of the most dangerous animals in Africa.

- Hippos can hold their breath underwater for five minutes or more. They probably need to because of the stink when their dung starts to fly. Only read the next fact if you've got a strong stomach and a peg on your nose...

- Brace yourself for the foulest hippo fact – hippopotamuses find any excuse to fling and toss their own poo around ... and they sometimes shoot it out of their mouths, like gross spitballs! If a male hippo backs out of the water towards you, take cover quick. It has a rotor-mixer tail that fires poo far and wide – like a giant turbo-charged muck-spreader. If that's not bad enough, all that splattered hippo poo is a tasty treat for others... baboons like to eat it. Don't they know doughnuts are nicer?

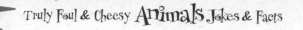

Silly Hippo Jokes

It may look like I'm laughing at the jokes. I'M NOT.

A teenager went to the zoo and smuggled out a baby hippo. He told his mum it was his only friend in the world and he'd keep it safe in his bedroom. His mum went bananas. 'Don't be ridiculous. What about the filth, foul smell and disgusting, horrible, nasty, revolting muck?'

'Who cares?' her son shrugged, 'the hippo will soon get used to it.'

A cowboy and his pet hippo walk into a saloon.

'Hey, bartender, get me a bath of water for my hippo.' The bartender brings out a tin bath and the hippo immediately gets in, lies on its back, gives a big yawn and goes to sleep – right in the middle of the room. The bartender, yells:

'Hey buddy, you can't just leave that lyin' there.'

The cowboy whispers, 'Sshh. Anyway, don't you know nothin'? That ain't no lion, that's a Hippopotamus.'

Hippo Riddles

Q: What do you call a hippo in a sports car?
A: Stuck

Q: What happens when a hippo gets too cold?
A: It suffers from hippothermia

Q: What do you call a hippo when it rolls in the mud and walks in the house?
A: A hippopota-mess

Q: What do you call a hippo with pondweed in one ear and thick mud in the other?
A: Anything you want – he can't hear you!

After all that elephant and hippopotamus dung, how about something less smelly? Alas, it's still poo time but even more gross. Now it's not so much smelly as tasty...

Poolicious

Did you know that many animals eat their own dung? How about a homemade fresh dinner for one? Some animals also eat other animals' dung so they just go out for a quick takeaway. 'Would you like flies with that?'

A surprising number of animals eat their own dung regularly. Rabbits, capybaras (the biggest rodent – from South America), gorillas, baby elephants, many insects and even dogs often chomp on their own droppings or on someone else's. Are they just badly brought up?

In fact, eating dung can give some animals another chance to get more nutrients from their food by recycling the old stuff. It's very similar to a cow chewing the cud (having a second bite at it), except that cows are able to re-eat their food without having to poo it out first.

Dogs and other animals will eat dung because it contains vitamins created by the bacteria that live in intestines. Also, dung can contain undigested protein. If you own both a dog and a cat, you may have noticed your dog making a dinner out of the cat's poo. This is because cat poo contains quite a lot of protein. But please don't try it at home – or anywhere else, for that matter.

Erm...nothing to do with me, I promise!

Did you know there are scientific names for the dung of different animals? See which of these 10 you know... or maybe test a friend with this 'match the poo' test. Warning: It's not easy – in fact, it's a real STINKER.

Bodewash	cows
Spraint	otters
Guano	seabirds
Frass	beetles
Billitting	foxes
Fumet	deer
Crotiles	hares
Lesses	wolves, bears and boars
Scumber	dogs
Buttons	sheep

Guano alert!

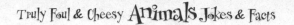

Warning: MAX STRENGTH STINK ALERT

Skunks

Skunks live throughout North America, especially in woodland areas in the United States, often near farms and even in cities. They're shy animals that don't want a fight, but if bothered, they've got a secret weapon up their sleeve (or more accurately, under their tail). They'll spray their enemies with a terrible sticky gunk that STINKS.

Something's wrong – I smell a rat.

Skunk Limerick

What an odorous creature the skunk is,
Far smellier than meerkats or monkeys.
With its secret device,
It's not very nice...
How disgusting its foul, stinky gunk is!

Phew - your stink is
so out of odour.

Skunk Joke

A duck, a skunk and a
deer went out for dinner at
a restaurant one night.
When it was time to pay,
the skunk didn't have a
scent and the deer didn't
have a buck, so they put
the meal on the duck's bill.

FOUR FOUL FACTS TO GIVE YOU NIGHTMARES

1 Skunks have glands in their bottom that spray their stinky smell up to 4 metres (12 feet) away. Apart from the vile smell lasting for days (or weeks and sometimes for months) the pongy spray is really irritating if it gets on your skin or in your eyes. It can even cause temporary blindness. But even if you're a long way from a squirty skunk, you could still know about it. People can smell the scent from anywhere up to a mile downwind.

2 Skunks live in old tree stumps or under logs. Sometimes they crawl into people's attics or basements. If there's a foul smell in your bedroom right now, it's best to take a peep under your bed, just in case.

3 The chemicals in 'skunk gunk' are called thiols – like the sulphur-based compounds found in garlic and onions. **WARNING:** these are also highly flammable – what you might call a skunk stink bomb. In the unlucky event that you or your dog gets sprayed by a skunk, soap and water won't get rid of the stink. It is said that sloshing yourself in tomato juice will get rid of the pong, but all you're really doing is just hiding it for a while.

4 To get rid of the smell once and for all, you need to alter the chemical makeup of the thiols, which you can do by getting a skunk deodorant containing a mixture of baking soda and hydrogen peroxide. Phew!

Am I making any scents?

What a stinker!

Q: How many skunks does it take to make a big stink?

A: Only a phew!

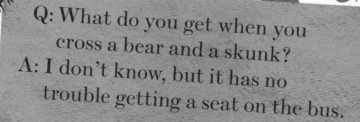

Q: What do you get when you
   cross a bear and a skunk?
A: I don't know, but it has no
   trouble getting a seat on the bus.

Q: How do you stop a
   skunk smelling so much?
A: Put a peg on its nose.

Stink

Skunk Joke

A policeman in the big city stopped a little old woman with a skunk on the front seat of her car.

'What are you doing with that filthy skunk?' he exclaimed. 'If that thing goes off you'll cause a real stink in this town. You should take it to the zoo.'

'Very well, officer,' she replied sweetly. 'I'll do as you say.'

The following week, the same policeman saw the same woman with the skunk still on the front seat, with both of them wearing sunglasses.

The policeman pulled them over.

'I thought you agreed to take that smelly thing to the zoo!'

The woman replied, 'Are you talking to me or the skunk, officer?'

'You, of course. I told you to take that animal to the zoo.'

'I did take it,' the woman smiled. 'I did exactly what you told me. We had a lovely time, and right now I'm taking it on another trip – to the beach.'

Reek

That joke stinks.

31

As Sick as a Parrot

Parrots aren't actually known for being sick over you. However, other birds seem to make it their main purpose to cough up foul-smelling sick whenever they feel like it.

The fulmar is a seabird of northern Europe, including the UK. The term fulmar means 'foul gull', and there's a good reason. Fulmar chicks are experts at projectile vomiting. When confronted by anything from eagles to gulls passing by, or unwary rock climbers, the fulmar chick will spit out a stinking oily mess all over the approaching face. How rude.

The roadrunner bird isn't quite like the cartoon character. It eats snakes, lizards and the odd tarantula. Although the roadrunner is fairly common across the south western United States, not many people know this bit... the chicks had better grow up fast or else. What happens to a roadrunner chick that doesn't gain weight fast enough? Mum simply throws it up in the air, opens her beak and GULP! End of.

A turkey vulture eats anything that's dead.
Very often it gorges itself on rotting meat and
becomes too heavy to fly off again. So if anything
threatens it while it's too fat to get away, it just
vomits everything all over whoever shows up.
This isn't just your average vomit, either. This
is vomit made from all the disgusting bits other
animals have left behind; this is rotting, maggot-
infested mega-yuk.

Oh, and another foul habit of the turkey vulture
you might not like to know...Apart from eating
rotting corpses, turkey vultures also wee down
their legs to cool themselves off. How delightful.

I'd take this away
but there's too much
carrion (carryin')

Vultures come in various shapes and sizes – none are the prettiest of birds (unless you happen to be another vulture). They have bald heads and necks so they can get stuck into sloppy guts and festering flesh without needing a feather stylist afterwards. Some vultures fly off with bones then drop them to smash them open and get to the yummy jelly bone marrow inside. Others prefer scrambled egg so they drop rocks onto ostrich eggs for a cracking good snack.

Penguin power can be amazing. That's not just the speed these birds can swim underwater – but the force of their projectile poo. Maybe it's the high fish diet or that penguins stand up straight – but when they poo, it's high pressure blasting. They poke their rears out and a max-strength jet of waste fires into the wind. Stand clear – or else...

I'm a super pooper!

34

Pelican Limerick

Have you seen the huge bill of the pelican
That holds as much fish as its belly can?
It gulps with a slurp
Then burps a loud BURP...
A bit like the way Great Aunt Nellie can!

Q: What do you call a parrot that
flew away?
A: A polygon

Q: What kind of mathematics do Snowy
Owls like most?
A: Owl-gebra

Q: What do you get if you cross a
cat with a parrot?
A: A carrot (or a cat with a feather in its
mouth and a satisfied smile)

Q: What kind of fish do pelicans like best?
A: Any kind – as long as it fits the bill

A duck waddled into a shop and quacked,
'Got any sweets?'
The shopkeeper snapped angrily,
'No. I don't serve ducks. Get out.'
The next day, the duck waddled back
into the same shop and asked the same
thing and got the same answer. The duck
kept going back every day for a week and
asked the same question but kept getting
the same answer. By the end of the week
the shopkeeper got so angry he shouted,
'If you come in here and ask that again,
I'll hit you on the head with a hammer!'
'You'll miss,' the duck said, 'because
I'll duck!'
*You might think that's the end of the
joke but there's more...*
The next day, the duck waddled back
into the shop and asked, 'Got a hammer?'
The shopkeeper screamed, 'No!'
The duck smiled and said, 'That's good.
Got any sweets?'

Hairy Scary Bears

A bear's sense of smell is so sharp it can detect animal carcasses upwind from 20 miles away. It could just as easily sniff food in your bag or a cheese roll in your pocket. If you haven't washed today and there's a bear within 20 miles right now... watch out!

I'll rip you apart with my BEAR hands.

Black Bears

Bear cubs may look cuddly and cute – but watch out for growly mum. She'll eat anything in autumn when she has to put on a lot of weight to see her through the long winter's hibernation. Unlike an average woman who eats about 1,600 calories a day, a female bear scoffs 15,000 calories per day. There's no telling what or who might be on her menu. In the last 100 years American black bears have killed well over 60 people (but not all at once).

Warning – if a black bear thinks you'd make a tasty snack, DON'T play dead. It will think you're dinner on a plate. It's best to wave your arms, make loud noises and try to fight it off. Good luck!

FOR THE RECORD: Not all American black bears are actually black as they can come in many shades from brown to blonde (almost white in parts of Canada).

Q: What colour socks do bears wear?
A: They don't wear socks, they have
   bear feet!

Q: What's black and white, black
   and white, and black and white?
A: Either a panda bear rolling down
   a hill or a penguin with a skunk
   on a zebra.

Q: What do you get if you cross a
   grizzly bear and a harp?
A: A bear-faced lyre!

Roar!

Rat 1: Stay safe in bear country by wearing little bells on your clothes.

Rat 2: Won't you get ringing wet?

Rat 1: Don't be daft. The jingling will warn bears that people are around.

Rat 2: What, like a dinner bell?

Rat 1: No. Bears attack when they're startled by loud noises. Also carry pepper spray, just in case.

Rat 2: Why? In case they like their food spicy?

I think life without bears would be unbearable.

Rat 1: Don't be daft. Always watch out for fresh signs of bears. Make sure you know the difference between black bear droppings and grizzly bear droppings.

Rat 2: So what's the difference?

Rat 1: Black bear droppings are smaller and contain lots of berries and squirrel fur.

Rat 2: Yeah – and grizzly bear droppings are larger, have little bells in it and smell like pepper.

Rat 1: Don't be daft. It's easy to tell which sort of bear is nearby.

Rat 2: Yeah – just go up to it, kick its behind then run up a tree.

Rat 1: How will that help?

Rat 2: If it climbs the tree and eats you, it's a black bear. If it knocks the tree down and eats you, it's a grizzly.

Rat 1: Doh!

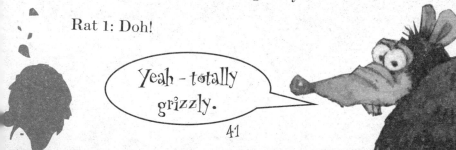

41

Grizzly Bears

Also called brown bears, 'grizzlies' can easily catch you if you try to run away. Playing dead and keeping still will show them you're not a threat. Grizzlies tend to attack if they feel threatened – rather than seeing you as dinner on legs. Even so, grizzly bears do kill to eat meat – they also eat berries and nuts, fish, rodents, elk and even moths. Yes, moths! These enormous bears are known to feast on army cutworm moths in Yellowstone Park. High in the mountains, these moths gather on rocks in their millions. Grizzlies climb the rocks to gulp down 10,000 to 20,000 moths a day. (Next time you think you've got butterflies in your tummy, remember the flutter-gut grizzly!)

A Grizzly Limerick

If you camp in the woods and it's drizzly,
It's best to fry-up something sizzly
But beware and keep looking
As the smell of your cooking
Might mean you wake up with a grizzly.
(When you're camping, always sleep with
your pants on. The only thing worse than a
bear in front of you is a BEAR BEHIND!)

What do you call a bear with no ear? B.

43

Polar Bears

The polar bear is the largest land-dwelling carnivore. The males are twice as big as females (the weight of 8–10 people or 4 lions). Although polar bears look white, the skin under their fur is actually black. Their hairs are hollow and appear white by reflecting the ice and snow off the Arctic. If you shave off all that fur (not a good idea unless the bear is up for it), you'll discover the polar bear's true colour. Under that shaggy coat, the polar bear's skin is black (to absorb heat from the sun and keep it warm). So the next time you see a polar bear's nose poking through the tent when you're camping in the Arctic, remember – that's its true colour!

A hungry polar bear can sniff out a seal's breathing hole in the ice from miles away. Seals are the biggest part of a polar bear's diet, but they have been known to eat people. People have also been known to eat them too – but be warned... There's one part of a polar bear you should never eat: the liver. It's so packed with vitamin A, it could kill you.

Gruesome Alert

Polar bears have been known to become cannibals. A mother polar bear might eat her cubs if they're sick. As the Arctic ice melts, polar bears become more desperate if trapped on dry land. Adult bears will sometimes eat younger bears – even their livers.

Polar Bear Limerick

A polar bear picked up the scent
Of a hiker asleep in his tent.
It popped in for a bite
And kissed him goodnight,
Gave a massive bear-hug, then it went.

Polar Bear Jokes

Q: Why are polar bears big,
   white and furry all over?
A: Because if they were
   white, small and smooth,
   they'd be aspirins.

Q: What did the polar bear eat after the dentist fixed its tooth?
A: The dentist!

Q: What do you get when you cross a polar bear with a red rose?
A: No idea – but whatever you do, don't try to sniff it.

A baby polar bear goes up to his mother and says, 'Mum, am I a real polar bear?' His mother says, 'Of course you're a real polar bear. I'm a polar bear and your father's a polar bear.' The cub says, 'But am I 100% pure polar bear?' She says, 'Your grandparents, both sides, were polar bears...yes, you're 100% pure polar bear. Why do you ask?" The cub says, 'Because I'm absolutely freezing.'

A polar bear went into a fish and chip shop. It strolled up to the counter and said, 'I'll have a large cod and chips and

....

a pickled onion.'
The woman behind the counter asked, 'Why the enormous pause?'
The polar bear shrugged and said, 'I dunno – I've always had them!'

Q: Why did the panda get fired from the circus?
A: It would only do the BEAR minimum.

Goldilocks and the Three Bears

Once upon a time there were three bears. They took a walk in the woods while their porridge cooled. When they get back they were amazed at what they saw.

Daddy bear said, 'Who's been eating my porridge?'

Mummy bear said, 'Who's been eating my porridge?'

Baby bear said, 'Never mind about the porridge – who's nicked the TV?'

Giant Panda Bears

Can you imagine eating the same thing all day, every day? Believe it or not, about 99% of a giant panda's diet is bamboo leaves and shoots. As bears have digestive systems designed to eat meat, there's not much nutrition in endless bamboo. No wonder pandas sit around a lot with a low-energy lifestyle – gobbling masses of bamboo each day just to stay full. That means chomping away for between 12 to16 hours of the day. But a diet so full of bamboo fibre has a downside. A panda poos big time – about the weight of a collie dog each day.

While on the exciting topic of panda poo—did you know scientists are looking into it? In fact, they're poking their noses right in it to understand how this large bear digests all that chewy, tough bamboo. By finding out what goes on in the bear's gut, they hope to develop new biofuels.

And another thing about panda poo... it makes a delicious brew of tea! Panda dung tea is grown in the mountains of China and is fertilized by the dung of giant pandas. In case you fancy a sip, it could cost you about $200 a cup. So if you take your tea black or white – try panda tea for a unique aroma and a taste of.... YUK.

Rat 1: What's black and white with red
spots and smells of bamboo?

Rat 2: A panda with measles.

Rat 1: Correct. What's yellow and
smells of bamboo?

Rat 2: Panda sick.

This is total panda-monium.

Rat 1: Correct. What's brown and smells of bamboo?

Rat 2: Does it also smell of poo?

Rat 1: Yes. You've guessed it. What's black and white and very noisy?

Rat 2: Easy – a panda with a drum kit. So what's green and smells of bamboo?

Rat 1: Oh no – not panda snot?

Rat 2: No. Bamboo.

I know what you call an exhausted bear after it's been to the toilet. Winnie the Pooped.

A Panda Joke

A panda walks into a restaurant and orders a bamboo sandwich. After munching it, the panda pulls out a gun and shoots a bottle on the counter and heads for the door.

'Hey!" shouts the waiter. 'Where are you going? You just shot and smashed a bottle without paying.' The panda yells back, 'Hey man, I am a **PANDA**! Look it up!'

The waiter opens a dictionary and reads what it says for panda: 'A black and white bear from Asia. Eats shoots and leaves.'

Bamboo sprouts are off the menu today.

Don't try to bamboozle me!

A Panda Limerick

My sister is Cuddly Amanda
(To be honest, I really can't
stand her)
She's extra large size,
With mascara eyes...
It's like sharing a house with
a panda.
(She likes bamboo sandwiches
as well)

When is a bear not a bear?

Just so you know... koala bears aren't really bears. They've got some gross habits so they deserve a mention. And yes, those habits do involve poo.

Baby koalas eat their own mothers' poo. Not just any poo – a specially made, creamy, extra wet kind of poo called pap. Pap contains gut bacteria that baby koalas need to survive before they can digest a diet of eucalyptus leaves. Cute little koalas lick their mums' bottoms to get their pap delivery. So if you ever get the chance to cuddle a sweet baby koala, you might not want to give it a kiss.

She's such a fussy eater!

Sloth bears live in the steamy jungles of Asia and love honey, but they can be super-aggressive and have even been known to beat up tigers. Sloths, on the other hand, are quite different and aren't bears at all. They are very slow tree-living mammals but get a mention here because they are totally DISGUSTING.

Two-toed sloths have added a new and tasty item to their diet: human poo. Scientists working in Peru have recorded sloths descending from trees at night to feed from toilet pits. For some sloths that's a great night out.

Sloths

The sloth is the world's slowest mammal, so slow that revolting plants grow on its furry coat. Slimy algae give the sloth a greenish tint in the trees of the South American rain forest. As it takes so long for a sloth to digest what it eats (leaves – and that gross stuff growing on its smelly body), it only 'goes to the toilet' about once a week, usually during the rare times it leaves the tree. A sloth's dirty rear end is just right for growing all that algae. In fact, the poo of three-toed sloths attracts moths that colonise sloth fur and help develop the 'algae gardens'. A sloth covered in gloppy green algae and moths looks a bit like a mouldy shag carpet on top of a compost heap. And if that's not bad enough, when it dies, a sloth often hangs around for a while. Their grip is so strong that sometimes when they die, sloths are found still clinging to the very branch they were dangling from when they were alive. Now they're DEAD slow.

You might be too slow to get this joke...
A sloth was hanging around in a tree when a gang of snails slid along the branch towards him. They beat him up and licked off all his algae for 7 hours. They left him lying in a heap at the bottom of a tree, covered in bruises and slime. Many hours later, the sloth managed to crawl away towards the police station. After a few days, he dragged himself onto the sergeant's desk.
'What happened to you?' an officer asked.
'A gang of snails beat me up,' the sloth replied.
'I'm shell-shocked.'
'Can you describe what they looked like?'
'I've got no idea,' the sloth replied after an hour.
'It all happened so fast.'

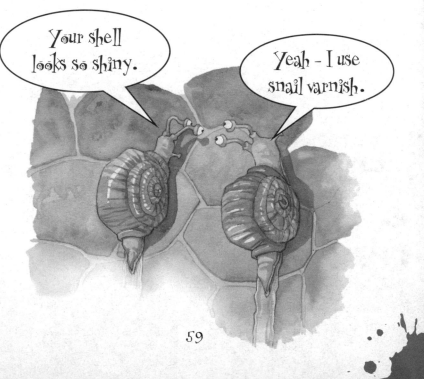

Your shell looks so shiny.

Yeah – I use snail varnish.

Big Cats

The male lion is known as the King of the Jungle – but he's more like the Slob of the Jungle. Most of the hunting work is done by the females while he flops about all day – resting for almost 20 hours a day. The lionesses have to hunt for him and let him eat first. Then he goes off to urinate all over the place to mark out his patch to say 'I'm the boss'.

Chomp Chomp

I'm taking you ladies out to dinner.

The menu looks grrrrrreat.

Apart from killing and gorging on prey, lions also scavenge up to 40 percent of their food by stealing it from other animals or by finding discarded animal carcasses. When an animal is killed, lions will eat virtually every part of it – the skin, meat, intestines, even the eyeballs. But they don't eat the stomach. It must smell really bad as lions often bury it.

Time to say grace...

Let us prey...

Q: What's the difference between a tiger and a lion ?
A: A tiger has the mane part missing!

Q: How do you take a lion's temperature?
A: Very carefully

Did you know...the lion's worst enemy is only the size of a small dog. The porcupine is the thorn in the big cat's side, or rather mouth. A lion tricked into sniffing the clever porcupine's sharp quills often ends up with one or more stuck in its jaw for life.

Try to eat me and you'll need a tranQUILLizer.

A boy walked into a restaurant with a lion on a lead. After being seated, he asked the waitress, 'Do you serve schoolboys here?' 'Yes, of course,' the waitress replied. 'Ok,' grinned the boy, 'I'll have some fries for me, and a schoolboy for my lion.'

How Catastrophic... Can you believe it? Some gardeners use lion dung (poo pellets) to put on their gardens to keep cats away. Mind you, it probably keeps everything away – including zebras and any passing elephants. It's probably great for growing dandelions!

I'd kill for a porcupine pizza.

63

Did you know…the roar of a lion can be heard from 5 miles (8 kilometres) away.

My birthday is in Ape-ril.

A zoo was having a bad day. The Head Bird Keeper found two dead finches in the aviary. Things were worse in the ape house where two chimpanzees had killed each other over a banana. The Lion Keeper collected the dead animals and threw them to the lions. One of the lions looked up from the dinner just landed at his feet and roared, 'Oh no – not Finch and Chimps!'

Did you know...When lions breed with tigers the offspring are known as ligers and tigons. There are also lion and leopard hybrids known as leopons. Lion and jaguar hybrids are known as jaglions.

There's no time for lion around.

Q: On which day do lions eat people?
A: Any day with a 'd' in it – especially Chewsday

Q: What's the difference between an injured lion and a wet day?
A: One pours with rain, the other roars with pain

A Lion Joke

A lion set off one morning to convince everyone he was King of the Beasts. He strode up to a monkey and roared, 'Who is the Mightiest of Animals?'

'You are, Master,' trembled the monkey. Then the lion went up to a warthog.

'Who is the Mightiest of Animals?' roared the lion.

'You are, my Lord,' quivered the warthog. Next the lion met an elephant. 'Who is the Mightiest of Animals?' roared the lion. The elephant grabbed the lion with his trunk, swung him in the air, slammed him against a tree trunk, threw him into a thorn bush, and strolled away.

'Okay!' shouted the lion. 'There's no need to turn nasty just because you don't know the answer!'

A Lion Limerick

A jungle explorer called Brian
Set off on his bike made of iron...
He returned from his ride
On the cosy inside
Of a lip-licking man-eating lion.
(Brian was a pioneer for
Meals on Wheels)

Tigers

Tigers are the largest wild cats in the world. Adults can weigh 360kg – that's about the same as 10 ten-year-olds. (11 ten-year-olds if it's just eaten one!) Every tiger in the world has unique markings – no two tigers have the same pattern of stripes. Did you know some tigers are white with blue eyes?

Did you know tigers can purr like pet cats? In fact, pet cats purr when they breathe in and out, and tigers can only purr when they breathe out. When tigers do purr, it's 100 times louder than a pet cat's purr…sounding a bit like a tractor stuck in the mud.

Tigers live and hunt alone. They quietly stalk their prey at night until they are close enough to pounce. They quickly kill their victim with a single bite to the neck or back of the head. Ouch. Apparently (in case you were wondering) a tiger's urine is said to smell like popcorn. Hmm... I wondered who was behind me in the cinema watching The Jungle Book and purring loudly.

If you think a tiger is about to attack you, try staring it straight in the eyes. Tigers prefer to hunt by ambush, so by staring back you are showing you know it's there so it's lost the upper hand (or paw). People in India sometimes wear face masks on the back of their heads to stop tigers creeping up on them from behind. Worth a try – although some tigers have figured out it's a trick... and pounced.

Fancy a snack?
How about human beings
on toast?

Rat 1: Did you know all tigers have different patterns? But they all have more stripes on one side than the other. Do you know which side a tiger has most stripes?

Rat 2: On the outside.

Rat 1: Correct. But did you hear who went into the tiger's den and actually came out alive?

Rat 2: Yeah – the tiger. Hey, what's striped and goes round and round?

Rat 1: Easy. A tiger in a revolving door.

Look out – there's a tiger behind you.

Rat 2: Did you hear about the stupid zookeeper in charge of the tigers? He named a baby tiger cub Spot.

Rat 1: Doh! Did you know a four legged animal is called a quadruped and a two-legged animal is a biped?

Rat 2: Yeah – and a tiger is a Stri-ped.

Rat 1: Doh!

Nah – it's just a lion in pyjamas.

Two men are walking through a forest when suddenly they see a tiger running towards them. They turn and make a dash for it but one of them stops suddenly, takes a pair of running shoes from his bag and starts to put them on.

'What are you doing?' screams his friend. 'Do you think you'll run faster than the tiger with those on?'

'Not at all – but I don't have to run faster than the tiger,' he says, darting off ahead. 'I just have to run faster than you.'

Roarrr!

A Terrifying Tale

At the end of the 1900s an injured tiger became one of the most dreaded man-eaters in Nepal. The female tiger killed 200 people and the army was sent to hunt her down. They failed to catch her and she escaped into India to continue her killing. It was said that with every human she killed, she became bolder and more fearless, and eventually, she started attacking in broad daylight and prowling around villages. A man called Jim Corbett followed a trail of blood and limbs from her latest victim. He shot the tigress in 1911 – by that time she had killed 436 humans. That tiger is still the most prolific individual man eater in history. Don't have nightmares...

Mmm...every human is tastier than the last!

The tiger's tongue is covered with many small, sharp, spiky bumps called papillae. These papillae give the tongue its rough, rasping surface to help strip the skin, feathers, fur and meat right off its prey. They have been known to lick the paint off the walls of their zoo enclosures. So it's best not to let a tiger lick your face!

You'll get the rough end of my tongue in a minute.

Look away now if you're squeamish. Tiger cubs are very cute-looking, right? Sometimes adult tigers will kill and eat them. Even parent tigers have become cannibals with their own young. It's unwise to annoy Mum if you're a tiger cub.

A Silly Poem

Some animals are cannibals and so is
my young cousin,
She'll eat men made of gingerbread and babies
by the dozen (jelly ones)
Just like a tiger, she'll pounce on top and
squash them underneath
Then bite each head off one by one to crush
between her teeth.
The gooey bits burst out and squelch with
every dribbling bite;
She licks her lips and wipes her chin and
purrs with sheer delight.
You'd think she was a tiger if you'd never
heard her purr before...
She's really vegetarian – a scary savage herbivore!

Leopards

Leopards don't tend to drink a lot as they get much of their moisture from their food – the blood of their prey. Gulp!

Smaller, more agile and maybe more cunning than lions or tigers, leopards were described as the deadliest animals in the world by big game hunters. One of them said, 'If the leopard was the size of a lion, it would be ten times more dangerous.'

So next time you spot a leopard, just hope it doesn't spot you. But spots are what make it a leopard!

A Spotty Riddle

Q: Why didn't the leopard cross the road?
A: He didn't want to get spotted.

A Scary Tail

The deadliest man-eating leopard of all time was the Panar leopard. This male leopard lived in India during the early 20th century and he killed over 400 people.

It seems that the leopard had been injured by a hunter, so was unable to hunt wild animals, so it turned to man-eating to survive.

I only eat people on a Chewsday.

When is a big(ish) cat not a cat?
When it's a palm civet cat (with a disgusting secret...)
Palm civets are not members of the cat family at all, but are more closely related to other small carnivores like mongooses. The African civet is famous for an oily musk it squeezes out of glands in its rear end. Both males and females squat and rub their bottoms on anything they can find to mark out their territory with a pongy paste. Would you believe – this 'bottom oil' has been used to make the most expensive perfumes for centuries. Nice.

But that's not the only yucky secret a civet has up its sleeve/bottom. Wait for it... do you fancy a cup of coffee? To be precise, civet coffee (called Kopi Luwak) is made by getting the animals to munch on coffee beans, then poo them out for a nice brew. The Asian civets digest the flesh of the coffee beans but poo out the beans inside. Their stomach juices work on the beans, adding to the coffee's prized aroma and flavour. Do you fancy a cup? Just one cup could cost you £80! Instead of 'fresh ground' it's more like 'fresh dung'. Mmmm, wake up and smell the coffee!

Time to work my magic...

By the way – a meerkat isn't a cat either. It's also related to the mongoose. Meerkats may seem fun animals but they have some horrible habits (apart from eating poisonous snakes). A meerkat will sometimes kill its 'less important' members of the group (called a 'mob', 'gang' or 'clan') to improve the position of its own offspring. Meerkats even take part in wrestling matches and other social activities (but not usually bingo or baseball).

Repulsive Reptiles

Reptiles are cold-blooded vertebrates (vertebrates have backbones). They have dry skin covered with scales or bony plates and usually lay soft-shelled eggs. Although there are around 6,000 different types of reptile, here are just a handful of foul facts to disturb you:

Tortoises are expert reptile survivors in hot deserts. Their hidden weapon is a mighty big bladder. A desert tortoise can hold over 40 percent of its body weight in its bladder where it stores water and revolting waste. Anyone who dares to attack a tortoise will get all that pee at full force.

My bladder is turtley full.

Snakes scare many people (especially if you have ophidiophobia). Although some snakes can be deadly if they bite you, the hognose snake is not likely to cause serious harm to humans. If you threaten one, it will pretend to be dead to make you leave it alone. Apart from flipping over on its back, opening its mouth and lying very still, it makes a foul smell to make you think it's rotting.

Hissssss

With a clue in its name, the African egg-eating snake adores eggs for breakfast. It will swallow an egg whole, and then use tiny spikes inside its body to crack the egg open and scramble up the insides before regurgitating the eggshell in a neatly folded parcel.

Lizards come in all shapes and sizes – the biggest being the komodo dragon. These venomous giants have been known to rob graves and eat human corpses, and they can also climb up ladders to get through windows and grab human prey.

Baby Komodo dragons are likely to get eaten by the adults, so they cover themselves in dung to make themselves less appetizing. Then they wait near a killed animal's intestines, camouflaged in dung, for a chance to take some meat for themselves. One day the little dragons will reach full size and be able to terrorize the next generation of Komodos – or anyone else who might be tasty.

You name it, I'll eat it.

Another lizard has a scary trick when it feels threatened. The horned lizard squirts blood from its eyes. Whoosh... Just imagine how that deals with any problem. (Please don't try this yourself in public.)

The alligator snapping turtle is the largest freshwater turtle in North America. With its spiked shell, beaklike jaws, and thick scaled tail, this species is often referred to as the 'dinosaur of the turtle world.' The alligator snapper has a bright red tongue like a worm to catch prey. When a fish or frog comes to take a look... SNAP! Its bite can instantly snap a broom handle – so watch out if you go swimming with a broom!

An elephant was drinking out of a pond when he spotted a snapping turtle asleep in the mud. He reached over with his trunk and threw it into the bushes.
'What did you do that for?' asked a passing hyena.
'Because that's the same turtle that took a nip out of my trunk 53 years ago.'
'Wow, what a memory!' the hyena gasped.
'Yes,' said the elephant. 'I've got TURTLE RECALL.'

Q: What do you call a sea turtle that flies?
A: A shell-icopter

Crash!

Q: What do you call a truck-load of tortoises crashing into a train-load of terrapins?
A: A turtle disaster.

Crocodiles

10 scary things you might not want to know about crocodiles...

1 99 percent of baby crocodiles get eaten in their first year – by large fish, herons, monitor lizards and adult crocodiles.

2 Crocodiles, which have been on earth for 240 million years, can live up to 80 years.

3 The largest crocodile species is the saltwater crocodile, living in eastern India, northern Australia and Southeast Asia. It can reach 7 metres long and weigh 1 tonne – so it's best not to pick a fight with one.

4 Crocs eat rocks! Fully grown adults can have a pile of stones in their stomachs. This not only helps them grind up and digest bones, but they also help weigh down the crocodiles' bodies underwater, where they lie in wait to attack.

5 A Nile crocodile can get through 50 sets of teeth in its life. It has 68 sharp teeth in all, but each tooth will fall out every year or so and a new one will grow. It's lucky for the crocodile that all its teeth don't fall out at the same time, or it would have to suck its prey to death!

6 'Crying crocodile tears' – which means to show fake sadness – comes from the myth that crocodiles weep when eating humans. They do wipe their eyes when feeding, but only because their eyes bubble and froth when eating. What terrible table manners.

7 In Africa alone there are several hundred crocodile attacks on humans per year. Many take place in small communities and are not widely reported. Between a third to half of attacks are fatal.

8 Crocodiles and alligators are slightly different. Crocodiles are larger, have V-shaped jaws and some of their teeth can be seen even when the jaw is fully closed. Alligators are smaller, they have U-shaped jaws and their teeth are not visible when their jaws are closed. But it's best not to take a close look to find out. Stare into the jaws of a crocodile or an alligator and it might be the last thing you see.

SNAP!

9 When it grabs very large prey, a crocodile drags it into the water to drown it. It does this by rolling over and over – called 'the death roll'. This spinning underwater is also how a crocodile will tear the limbs from the body of large prey... twisting and turning until it can rip off chunks of its victim for gulping down.

10 Gustave is a large male Nile crocodile in Burundi, Africa. He is thought to be over 60 years old and is a man-eater – having killed as many as 300 humans from the banks of the Ruzizi River and the northern shores of Lake Tanganyika. He is greatly feared by people in the region, who say he kills as much for fun as for food – often killing several people in every attack. He then disappears for months before appearing somewhere else. So look out for Gustave next time you go for a swim (wherever it may be) – just in case.

Rat 1: What does a crocodile call a giraffe with three legs?

Rat 2: Lunch.

Rat 1: What does a crocodile call a giraffe with two legs?

Rat 2: Leftovers.

Rat 1: What does a crocodile call a giraffe with four legs?

Rat 2: The one that got away.

Rat 1: What does a giraffe call a crocodile blocking its way in the river?

Rat 2: Sir

Rat 1: What's the best thing to do if you find a crocodile in your bed?

Rat 2: Sleep somewhere else.

Rat 1: What do you call a crocodile spy in a vest?

Rat 2: I don't know, what do you call a crocodile spy in a vest?

Rat 1: A private in-vest-i-GATOR.

Rat 2: Doh!

These jokes are even too cheesy for me!

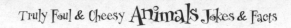

An Ode to Gustave: Snap, Crackle, Croc!

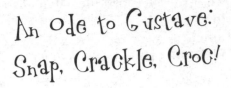

Never mock the killer croc
Whose jaws unlock behind the rock
To crack snap-shut in shock headlock.
He's chock-a-block by one o'clock.

But Mrs. Spock said, 'Poppycock!'
And with a hop got on the rock.
'Come on,' she scoffed, 'Chop-chop,
chop-chop!'
So Gustave did.

Let's go for a bite.
Hurry up - make it snappy.

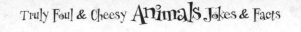

Off went her frock (pink hollyhock),
Mock croc-skin shoe and cotton sock.
With rock and roll, and roll and rock,
He knocked her like a shuttlecock.

She scoffed and so he scoffed her up… bless her.

She was to the end such a **SNAPPY** dresser.
Her rainbow scarf was all they found…
Stuck on his tooth with her gold ring crowned.

Just dry those crocodile tears and try to smile,
He crunched her eighteen carat ring and striped silk
  scarf with style.
Expensive taste, but it's truth that must be told….
At the end of every rainbow, there lies a croc of gold!

Monkey Business

You might think it's disgusting, but many apes and monkeys eat ticks and fleas they pick off their friends' hairy bodies. In fact, it's a friendly way of grooming each other. By picking off the itchy bugs and swallowing them, monkeys not only get rid of pests but they do their friends a favour and get to bond with them. Everyone's a winner – apart from the fleas.

Help - I've got fleas all over me.

They're only itch-hiking.

96

A Monkey Limerick

If you've got a fluorescent pink bottom
(Let's face it, some monkeys have got 'em)
Would you squat on the floor,
Make your buttocks red-raw
Just so tourists queue daily to spot 'em?
(It's the main attraction in some zoos!)

Stop all this monkey business.

If your life is in need of a thriller,
It's best not to visit a killer...
Whatever you do,
Don't pop down the zoo

With a banana to poke a gorilla!
(or it could go APE)

A baboon with disgusting behind
Sat splat on the windscreen and whined.
The driver looked glum
At the squashed purple bum
And protested, 'Hey, do you mind?'

An orang-utan up in the trees
Swung upside down on a trapeze.
The safari park staff
Squealed a horrified laugh
When it pooed on the Board of Trustees.

I love all this monkeying around.

A chimpanzee with a sweet smile
Stooped down for a drink from The Nile.
She stared with affection
At her grinning reflection...
SNAP! Alas, 'twas a huge crocodile.

Giraffe

A giraffe has a really long bluish black tongue that it uses for picking its nose and cleaning out its ears. If that isn't yucky enough, just check out its body odour and personal hygiene problem. Having such a long neck makes grooming tricky, so its skin releases chemicals to repel insects and disinfect the skin against fungi and bacteria. This chemical cocktail leaves a giraffe's skin smelling revolting to humans. Some older giraffes are so saturated with the foul pong that local people can smell them a long way off and call them 'stink bulls'.

Eating from tall trees can be a pain in the neck.

Q: What's green and hangs from trees?
A: Giraffe snot.

Q: What do you get when you cross a giraffe with a hedgehog?
A: A four-metre toothbrush.

Q: How can you tell if a giraffe has been in your fridge?
A: Hoof-prints in the trifle and all your Acacia leaves are missing.

101

Camel

Camels can kick in all four directions with each of their legs (but not at the same time!). One of the camel's foulest habits is "spitting" – with scary force and perfect aim. It throws up a foul smelling greenish fluid from its stomach all over you if you upset it. And just for the record – it might seem gross, but camel milk is amazing stuff. It has 10 times more iron and three times more vitamin C than cow's milk. If you fancy a camel milkshake, just give a camel a pogo stick for five minutes.
Oh yes, and camel urine can be as thick as syrup (but best not pour it on ice cream).

Cow

There are about 1.5 billion cows on the planet – all grazing, sleeping, chewing their cud, pooing and releasing gas. When cows digest food, it ferments inside them and makes massive amounts of methane gas every day. That's a lot of belching and farting which adds to greenhouse gases and global warming. So do the gases and ammonia in cow dung. Added up, burps from cows account for 26 percent of the United States' total methane emissions. You probably didn't want to know that.

I'm in a really happy moo-ed.

Q: What did mother cow say to baby cow?
A: It's pasture bedtime.

Q: What do you call a cow that comes into your garden to eat the grass?
A: A lawn moo-er.

Q: What do you get when you cross an octopus and a cow?
A: An animal that can milk itself.

It's time to turn the udder cheek and moo-ve on.

Frog

A frog that grows hair might seem freaky enough, but the hairy frog (also known as 'the horror frog') has another scary habit if it has to defend itself. Not having claws, it's come up with a way to scratch its way out of trouble. How? The frog snaps its front legs and pokes out its broken bones through the skin on its feet – just so it can lash out. How gross is that?

Q: What kind of shoes does
the hairy frog wear?
A: Open toad sandals!

When I meet a lady
frog I get tongue-tied.

Bats

Vampire bats only hunt at night and have teeth so sharp that their bite is virtually painless. They don't actually suck blood but lap it up with their tongue. Their special saliva keeps the blood flowing and stops it from clotting – as they don't like lumpy drinks! A vampire bat drinks blood at one end of its body, so its other end is peeing all the time to keep them light enough to take off in a hurry. Sometimes they fly off to spit blood out again for a friend to drink. How cute.

Fangs for having me.

However, vampire bats do have a rather nasty habit that might freak you out. Scientists aren't quite sure why, but vampire bats tend to feed on the same victim night after night, and they seem to be able to recognise an individual human just by the sound of their breathing. That means if you're ever bitten by a bat and it happens to think you're extra tasty, it will seek you out again by remembering the exact sound of your breath. Spooky, or what?

Q: Did you hear about the two bats meeting?
A: It was love at first bite.

Q: What is a vampire bat's favourite dessert?
A: I-Scream!

Kangaroos

A baby kangaroo is only the size of a jelly bean when it is born and looks like a tiny, pink, hairless, worm. As it grows in its mother's pouch, the baby joey pees and poos inside, so mum has to keep licking it all out. Kangaroo breath must be gross – and apparently the grey kangaroo males have a strong smell like curry. A vindaloo kangaroo?

Q: Where does a kangaroo
go to get new glasses?

A: The Hoptician.

Rat 1: Not many people like us, you know. It's not fair.

Rat 2: Don't get so ratty about it.

Rat 1: Do you know why?

Rat 2: Yeah – they say we spread disease because we live in sewers.

Rat 1: I don't live in a sewer. I'm an upper class rat.

Rat 2: Yeah. We live in the grand town hall.

Rat 1: In the toilets. Did you know a rat can tread water for three days?

Rat 2: Yeah – I do it all the time when I get flushed down the toilet.

Don't get ratty with me.

Rat 1: Did you know rats can fall 16 metres and land unharmed?

Rat 2: Yeah – I do that all the time then climb back up the wall.

Rat 1: Did you know rats' front teeth grow 12-14 centimetres (4½ to 5½ inches) in a year?

Rat 2: Yeah – that's why we're always gnawing at stuff to wear them down.

Rat 1: I can't stop chewing; cement, brick, wood, lead pipes, poo...

Rat 2: I can't think why people don't like us.

Rat 1: They're just jealous of all our babies.

Rat 2: Yeah – I've just counted... we've had 2,000 this year.

I'm just worn out, that's all. Life's a rat race right now.

113

Rat 1: Hey, do you fancy some cheese?

Rat 2: Have you chewed through the back of the fridge again?

Rat 1: Yeah – I went on a raid. I got some nice cheddar and I peed in the butter.

Rat 2: I love you – you're so cheesy and foul.

Rat 1: I do my best.

Rat 2: It's so cool being a rat. We ought to be in a book.

Rat 1: Don't be daft. No one would want to read foul and cheesy stuff.

Rat 2: Doh!

The trouble with being in the rat race is that, even if you win, you're still a rat.

And Finally...

In the time it has taken you to read this book, millions of little mouths have been chomping away on the world's steaming mega-tonnes of manure. At the same time, mountains of fresh supplies have plopped onto the earth – ready to be recycled for the next generation of animals. That may seem foul to you – but to any dung beetles or rats reading this, it's totally **POOTASTIC!**

QUIZ

1. In the wild, what do dung beetles use elephant poo for?

a) Building weapons

b) Building nests

c) Building waterslides

2. What do skunks do when they feel scared or threatened?

a) They become camouflaged

b) They spray a horrible, smelly gunk at their enemies

c) They do a silly dance to confuse the enemy

3. What animal uses projectile vomiting as a form of defence?

a) Red ants

b) The fulmar bird

c) Human babies

4. What should you do if you run into a grizzly bear?

a) Invite him round for tea

b) Give him a cuddle to calm him down

c) Play dead

5. A polar bear's fur is colourless. Why does it appear to be white?

a) It reflects off the snow

b) It's a fashion statement

c) The snow sticks to them

6. What is a lion's worst enemy?

a) An elephant

b) A giraffe

c) A porcupine

Mind if I stick my neck out?

7. What is the tortoises' ultimate weapon?

a) An extendable neck that is used to knock out enemies when the tortoise feels threatened

b) A shell which shoots out tiny blades on attack

c) A big bladder

Neck-st question, please!

8. Why are giraffes also known as 'stink bulls' by the local people?

a) The giraffe has a smelly self-cleaning mechanism that disinfects the skin

b) They have two tiny horns on their head

c) They hang around with bulls all the time

10. Why do dogs like to eat cat poo?

a) Because it's delicious (haven't you tried it?)

b) It contains lots of protein

c) It is a way to calm them down when they feel stressed

How many did you guess right?

Answers:

1 = b
2 = b
3 = b
4 = c
5 = a
6 = c
7 = c
8 = a
9 = c
10 = b

GLOSSARY

Algae: types of plant-like organism that typically live in the water and use photosynthesis to survive.

Bacteria: microscopic lifeforms, which are usually single-celled and often cause disease.

Bone marrow: soft, jelly-like tissue inside the bones which forms new blood cells for the body.

Hibernation: when certain species of animal go to sleep for an extended period of time, lowering their body temperature, in order to survive the winter months when little food is available.

Intestines: the digestive system between the stomach and anus, where the nutrients from food are absorbed into the body.

Nutrients: substances that living organisms obtain from their food or the surrounding environment in order to live and grow.

Protein: nutritional substance obtained by living organisms through food that helps them carry out the chemical processes needed to go on living.

INDEX

I finished reading this Truly
Foul & Cheesy book on:

........../........../..........